CW01508827

Test Your Kr
Through Boston Red
Sox Trivia and
Quizzes

History of Baseball Team Boston Red Sox and Simple Quiz Around Team

Copyright © 2021

DEDICATION

Contents

Boston Red Sox

The Boston Red Sox are an American professional baseball team based in Boston, Massachusetts. They compete in Major League Baseball (MLB) as a member club of the American League (AL) East division. The team have won nine World Series championships, tied for the third-most of any MLB team, and they have played in 14. Their most recent World Series appearance and win was in 2018. In addition, they won the 1904 American League pennant, but were not able to defend their 1903 World Series championship when the New York Giants refused to participate in the 1904 World Series. Founded in 1901 as one of the American League's eight charter franchises, the Red Sox' home ballpark has been Fenway Park since 1912. The "Red Sox" name was chosen by the team owner, John I. Taylor, circa 1908, following the lead of previous teams that had been known as the "Boston Red Stockings", including the forerunner of the Atlanta Braves.

The Red Sox were a dominant team in the new league, defeating the Pittsburgh Pirates in the first World Series in 1903 and winning four more championships by 1918. However, they then went into one of the longest championship droughts in baseball history, dubbed the

"Curse of the Bambino" after its alleged inception due to the Red Sox' sale of Babe Ruth to the rival New York Yankees two years after their world championship in 1918, an 86-year wait before the team's sixth World Championship in 2004. The team's history during that period was punctuated with some of the most memorable moments in World Series history, including Enos Slaughter's "mad dash" in 1946, the "Impossible Dream" of 1967, Carlton Fisk's home run in 1975, and Bill Buckner's error in 1986. Following their victory in the 2018 World Series, they became the first team to win four World Series trophies in the 21st century, with championships in 2004, 2007, 2013 and 2018. The team's history has also been marked by the team's intense rivalry with the New York Yankees, arguably the fiercest and most historic in North American professional sports.[3][4][5]

The Boston Red Sox are owned by Fenway Sports Group, which also owns Liverpool F.C. of the Premier League in England. They are consistently one of the top MLB teams in average road attendance, while the small capacity of Fenway Park prevents them from leading in overall attendance.[6] From May 15, 2003 to April 10, 2013, the Red Sox sold out every home game—a total of 820 games (794 regular season) for a major professional sports record.[7][8] Both Neil Diamond's "Sweet Caroline" and The Standells's "Dirty Water" have become anthems for the Red Sox.[9][10]

As of the end of the 2020 season, the Red Sox all-time record is 9,626–8,944 (.518)

Trivia Quiz - History of the Red Sox

1. What stadium did the Red Sox call home for the majority of the 20th century?

Huntington Avenue Baseball Grounds

Fenway Park

Boston Stadium

Red Sox Field

2. Babe Ruth played for the Red Sox from 1914-1919. Which team was he sent to in 1920?

Cleveland Indians

Chicago Cubs

New York Yankees

Cincinnati Reds

3. Which player that played for the Red Sox from 1907-1915 was inducted into the Hall of Fame in 1937?

Nap Lajoie

Tris Speaker

Ty Cobb

Babe Ruth

4. How many times in the 1910s did the Red Sox win the World Series?

3

5

2

4

5. Which former Red Sox player managed them in 1963 and 1964?

Johnny Pesky

Bobby Doerr

Ted Williams

Dom DiMaggio

6. Which pitcher became the first Red Sox pitcher to win the Cy Young Award in 1967?

Gary Bell

Jose Santiago

Jim Lonborg

John Wyatt

7. The Red Sox are often remembered for winning game 6 of the 1975 World Series with a walk-off home run in the bottom of the 12th inning. But do you know what player hit that home run?

Carl Yastrzemski

Bernie Carbo

Fred Lynn

Carlton Fisk

8. Which Red Sox player let a ground ball roll through his legs, which eventually led to the Red Sox losing the 1986 World Series?

Ed Romero

Wade Boggs

Bill Buckner

Marty Barrett

9. Which Red Sox player that they acquired in 2003, was often referred to by his nickname "Big Papi"?

Manny Ramirez

David Ortiz

Nomar Garciaparra

Bill Mueller

10. When the Red Sox won the 2004 World Series, how many years had it been since they had won their previous championship?

75

86

98

62

ANSWERS

1. What stadium did the Red Sox call home for the majority of the

20th century?

The correct answer was Fenway Park

Fenway Park is famous for its nearly 40-foot tall wall in left field, nicknamed "The Green Monster" for its green color. Although the wall is very high, it is only 310 feet from home plate.

2. Babe Ruth played for the Red Sox from 1914-1919. Which team was he sent to in 1920?

The correct answer was New York Yankees

Ruth was sent there a little over a year after leading the Red Sox to a World Series championship in 1918. He supposedly started the "Curse of the Bambino", because it took the Red Sox more than 80 years afterwards to win the World Series again.

3. Which player that played for the Red Sox from 1907-1915 was inducted into the Hall of Fame in 1937?

Answer: Tris Speaker

Speaker retired as the MLB career leader in doubles with 792, and 241 of them came while playing with the Red Sox.

4. How many times in the 1910s did the Red Sox win the World Series?

The correct answer was 4

They won the 1912, 1915, 1916, and 1918 World Series.

5. Which former Red Sox player managed them in 1963 and 1964?

The correct answer was Johnny Pesky

Pesky was a player for the Red Sox in 1942, 1946-1951, and part of the 1952 season.

6. Which pitcher became the first Red Sox pitcher to win the Cy Young Award in 1967?

The correct answer was Jim Lonborg

That year, Lonborg had a 22-9 record and led the American League in wins and games started (39). Lonborg played seven seasons for the Red Sox (1965-1971) before playing a season with the Milwaukee Brewers, and seven seasons with the Philadelphia Phillies (1973-1979) before retiring.

7. The Red Sox are often remembered for winning game 6 of the 1975 World Series with a walk-off home run in the bottom of the 12th inning. But do you know what player hit that home run?
Answer: Carlton Fisk

The Red Sox were playing the Cincinnati Reds in that World Series. Fisk hit a deep fly ball that hit the left field foul pole next to the Green Monster. The Reds went on to win game 7 and the World Series.

8. Which Red Sox player let a ground ball roll through his legs, which eventually led to the Red Sox losing the 1986 World Series?
The correct answer was Bill Buckner

The Red Sox were playing the New York Mets in the World Series. There were two outs in the bottom of the tenth inning in game 6. If Buckner had taken the ground ball at first base and touched first, it would have ended the inning and extended the game. However, since he let the ball roll through his legs, the Mets scored the winning run, and won the series in game 7 two days later.

9. Which Red Sox player that they acquired in 2003, was often referred to by his nickname "Big Papi"?
The correct answer was David Ortiz

Before going to the Red Sox, Ortiz played for the Minnesota Twins from 1997-2002. He signed as a free agent with the Red Sox in 2003, and the next year, helped the Red Sox to the World Series title.

10. When the Red Sox won the 2004 World Series, how many years had it been since they had won their previous championship?
Answer: 86

In the American League Championship Series, the Red Sox became the first team in baseball history to come back from a 3 games to none deficit and still win the series. This title ended the "Curse of the Bambino", the supposed "curse" that began when Babe Ruth left the Red Sox.

Trivia Quiz - The Impossible Dream

1. Who managed the Boston Red Sox to the 1967 American League pennant?

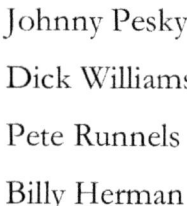

Johnny Pesky

Dick Williams

Pete Runnels

Billy Herman

2. Carl Yastrzemski won the American League's Triple Crown in 1967. Which slugger tied Yaz's mark of 44 home runs that season?

Harmon Killebrew

Al Kaline

Frank Robinson

Frank Howard

3. Which pitcher on the 1967 Boston Red Sox led the team in wins?

Jim Lonborg

Lee Stange

Jose Santiago

Gary Bell

4. On April 14, 1967, rookie Red Sox hurler Billy Rohr nearly pitched a no-hitter at Yankee Stadium. Which Yankees player broke up Rohr's no-hit bid in the ninth inning?

Bill Robinson

Mickey Mantle

Elston Howard

Horace Clarke

5. Infielder Jerry Adair was an important player on the 1967 Red Sox. Which American League team traded him to the Bosox?

Baltimore Orioles

Chicago White Sox

Kansas City A's

California Angels

6. Which of these teams was not a contender in the 1967 American

13

League pennant chase?

Chicago White Sox
Detroit Tigers
Minnesota Twins
New York Yankees

7. On August 18, 1967, star Boston outfielder Tony Conigliaro was seriously injured after getting hit by a wild pitch. Which Angels' pitcher beaned Conigliaro?

Clyde Wright
George Brunet
Jack Hamilton
Minnie Rojas

8. George Scott was a hard-hitting and smooth-fielding member of the 1967 Boston Red Sox. Which uniform number did he wear?

2
40

3

5

9. Which pitcher led the 1967 Boston Red Sox with 20 saves?

Sparky Lyle

John Wyatt

Darrell Brandon

Dan Osinski

10. During the 1967 World Series, two members of the Red Sox had two home run games against the Cardinals. One was Carl Yastrzemski. Who else performed the feat?

Rico Petrocelli

Joe Foy

Reggie Smith

Jose Tartabull

ANSWERS

1. Who managed the Boston Red Sox to the 1967 American League pennant?

The correct answer was Dick Williams

Dick Williams was a rookie manager when he led the Red Sox to a title in 1967. He was a no-nonsense leader who demanded hard work and hustle from his players. Williams managed the Red Sox from 1967 to 1969, and he ended up with 1575 victories during his Hall of Fame career. Billy Herman and Pete Runnels managed the Bosox during the 1966 season and Pesky was Boston's manager from 1963 to 1964. Pesky also managed the Red Sox for a short period in 1980.

2. Carl Yastrzemski won the American League's Triple Crown in 1967. Which slugger tied Yaz's mark of 44 home runs that season?

The correct answer was Harmon Killebrew

Carl Yastrzemski had a legendary season for the Red Sox, hitting 44 home runs, knocking home 121 runs, and batting .328. Harmon Killebrew of the Minnesota Twins also belted 44 home runs in 1967. Frank Robinson of the Orioles, winner of the Triple Crown in 1966, had 30 HRs. Frank Howard of the Senators hit 36 HRs, and Al Kaline blasted 25 HRs for the Tigers.

3. Which pitcher on the 1967 Boston Red Sox led the team in wins?
The correct answer was Jim Lonborg

Jim Lonborg won the 1967 American League Cy Young award, going 22-9 for the season. He also had two victories against the St. Louis Cardinals in the 1967 World Series. Bell and Santiago had 12 victories each for Boston, and Stange won eight games.

4. On April 14, 1967, rookie Red Sox hurler Billy Rohr nearly pitched a no-hitter at Yankee Stadium. Which Yankees player broke up Rohr's no-hit bid in the ninth inning?
The correct answer was Elston Howard

Elston Howard, an all-star catcher for many seasons, lined a single against Rohr with two outs in the bottom of the ninth inning. Howard would later join the 1967 Red Sox in a late-season deal. Billy Rohr's career didn't last very long. He pitched in only 10 games in 1967, winning two and losing three with an ERA of 5.10.

5. Infielder Jerry Adair was an important player on the 1967 Red Sox. Which American League team traded him to the Bosox?
The correct answer was Chicago White Sox

Jerry Adair was a veteran infielder who provided leadership, fielding prowess, and clutch hitting for the Red Sox. He had three home runs, knocked home 26 runs and batted .291 for Boston in 1967. The Red Sox acquired Adair from the White Sox on June 2, 1967, in exchange for pitcher Don McMahon.

6. Which of these teams was not a contender in the 1967 American League pennant chase?
The correct answer was New York Yankees

The 1967 American League pennant race was amazing. Four teams had a chance to win the title going into the last week of the season. Boston finished with 92 victories. The Twins and the Tigers ended up with 91 wins each, and Chicago had 89 victories. The Yankees had a woeful season, going 72-90 for a ninth-place finish.

7. On August 18, 1967, star Boston outfielder Tony Conigliaro was seriously injured after getting hit by a wild pitch. Which Angels' pitcher beaned Conigliaro?

The correct answer was Jack Hamilton

Tony Conigliaro was having a terrific season with Boston until the beaning. He had 20 HRs, 67 RBIs and batted .287 for the year. He suffered a broken cheekbone and serious eye damage. Hamilton was a hard-throwing right-handed pitcher for the Angels. He insisted that he was not a "head hunter". Conigliaro returned to Major League baseball and won Comeback Player of the Year honors in 1969.

8. George Scott was a hard-hitting and smooth-fielding member of the 1967 Boston Red Sox. Which uniform number did he wear?

The correct answer was 5

George "Boomer" Scott had a fine 1967 season for the Red Sox, hitting .303 with 19 home runs and 82 RBIs. During his career, Scott smashed 271 home runs, 154 of them with Boston. Mike Andrews wore number 2 for the Red Sox, Dalton Jones was in the number 3 uniform, and Ken Harrelson wore number 40.

9. Which pitcher led the 1967 Boston Red Sox with 20 saves?

The correct answer was John Wyatt

John Wyatt pitched in the big leagues from 1961 to 1969, earning 103 saves. He worked with the Red Sox from 1966 to 1968. Sparky Lyle notched five saves for Boston in 1967. Brandon had three saves and Osinski ended up with two.

10. During the 1967 World Series, two members of the Red Sox had two home run games against the Cardinals. One was Carl Yastrzemski. Who else performed the feat?

The correct answer was Rico Petrocelli

On October 11, 1967, shortstop Rico Petrocelli hit a pair of home runs off St. Louis pitcher Dick Hughes to lead the Red Sox to an 8-4 victory at Fenway Park. Reggie Smith and Carl Yastrzemski also homered in that game. Petrocelli would end his Boston career (1963-1976) with 210 home runs.

Trivia Quiz - A Fairly Biased Quiz

1. Who missplayed a ground ball in the game 6 of the 1986 World Series that allowed the game winning run for the Mets?

Dave Henderson

Marty Barrett

Don Baylor

Bill Buckner

2. Who did the Red Sox sell in the offseason of 1919-1920 to the Yankees?

Carl Mays

Ty Cobb

Babe Ruth

Mike McNally

3. In what year did the Boston Red Sox win their first world series?

1915

1918

1903

1912

4. In what year was Fenway Park first used as the Boston Red Sox's home stadium?

1912

1901

1918

1905

5. Before Boston used moved to Fenway Park, what was their previous home stadium?

South End Grounds

McCoy Stadium

Congress Street Grounds

Huntington Avenue Grounds

6. Which of these four had the highest single-season batting average at the Red Sox?

Ted Williams

Carl Yastrzemski

Babe Ruth

Joe Cronin

7. From 1901 to 1907, the Boston Red Sox were actually known by a different name. What was it?

Boston Beaneaters

Boston Braves

Boston Royals

Boston Americans

8. During what is known as "The Curse of the Bambino", how many times did the Red Sox make the World Series but fail to win?

6

5

4

3

9. Which pitcher was the first to ever pitch twenty strikeouts in a single nine inning game and was one of Boston greatest pitchers ever?

Cy Young

Roger Clemens

Carl Mays

Timn Wakefield

10. Who was the first person to pitch for Boston in 1901 and is considered the greatest pitcher ever?

Cy Young

Jake Molz

Ben Beville

Christy Matthewson

ANSWERS

1. Who missplayed a ground ball in the game 6 of the 1986 World Series that allowed the game winning run for the Mets?

The correct answer was Bill Buckner

In game 6 of the 1986 World Series, the Mets came back to tie the game in the tenth inning. With two outs, Mookie Wilson of the Mets comes up and hits a slow roller in the direction of Buckner. Buckner rushes the play and misses the ball with his glove causing it to roll into right field and allow Ray Knight, who was on second, to score the game winning run. The Sox then lost game seven, kepping the "Curse of the Bambino" alive.

2. Who did the Red Sox sell in the offseason of 1919-1920 to the Yankees?

The correct answer was Babe Ruth

Babe Ruth, also known as "The Bambino", was sold to the Yankees before the start of the 1920 season. Boston regretted this decision (Babe Ruth had just broken the single season HR record with 29 dingers) as Babe Ruth went on to top the all-time home run list and become one of the greatest players ever. This trade supposedly sparked what is known as "The Curse of the Bamnino", a period of 84 years where the Red Sox never won a world series (from 1918 to 2004).

3. In what year did the Boston Red Sox win their first world series?

The correct answer was 1903

Not only did the Red Sox win their first World Series in 1903, by beating the Pittsburgh Pirates, but that was also the first ever world series. All those other years were also years that Boston won the World Series. In 1912, they beat the New York Giants. In 1915, they beat the Philladelphia Phillies. And in 1918, led by Babe Ruth, they beat the Chicago Cubs.

4. In what year was Fenway Park first used as the Boston Red Sox's home stadium?
Answer: 1912

Fenway Park, famous for its infamous "Green Monster", is located in downtown Boston, Massachusetts and has been used since 1912. It has some pretty famous places in it like the already mentioned Green Monster and "The Lone Red Seat". "The Lone Red Seat" is located 502 ft. away from Home plate in right field. It marks the spot where the longest home run ever hit in Fenway Park landed (hit by Ted Williams on June 9, 1946). It bounced off spectator's head - Joseph A. Boucher.

5. Before Boston used moved to Fenway Park, what was their previous home stadium?

The correct answer was Huntington Avenue Grounds

The Huntington Avenue Grounds were used from 1901 to 1911 as the Red Sox's home field. If it was still around today, it would be one of the biggest ballparks around, not by capacity but by field size. At one point, the center field wall was 635 feet away from the plate! It was also the location of the first pitch and perfect game in MLB's "modern era" (post 1901 after AL was formed). Both was done by the famous Cy Young (the perfect pitch was on May 5, 1904 pitching for the Red Sox vs. Philadelphia Athletics).

6. Which of these four had the highest single-season batting average at the Red Sox?

The correct answer was Ted Williams

Ted Williams played for the Red Sox from 1936 to 1960 (missing the 1943, 1944, and 1945 seasons due to serving in the WWII). He had their highest single season batting average of .406 (in 1941) and a career batting average of .344. He was inducted into the Baseball Hall of Fame in 1966, his first year of eligibility. His number 9 was retired by the Red Sox in 1984.

7. From 1901 to 1907, the Boston Red Sox were actually known by a different name. What was it?

The correct answer was Boston Americans

The Boston Red Sox franchise was formed in 1901 as the Boston Americans. They won their first World Series in 1903 (the franchise changed its name in 1908). The Boston Beaneaters was actually a previous name of the Boston Braves who later moved to Atlanta. The Boston Royals were a team who played in the Negro League.

8. During what is known as "The Curse of the Bambino", how many times did the Red Sox make the World Series but fail to win?

The correct answer was 4

In 1946, Boston made it to the World Series for the first time since the Babe was traded in 1919. The team, led by Ted Williams, lost in a seven game series against the St. Louis Cardinals. In 1967, they made it again, this time led by Carl Yastrzemski. They again lost to the St. Louis Cardinals in a seven game series. In 1975, they made the World Series, this time to face the Cincinatti Reds. Led again by Carl and Carlton Fisk, they lost in another seven game series. Finally, in 1986, they made the Series to play the New York Mets. This was the year of the famous Bill Buckner slip up and Boston lost in ANOTHER seven game series.
The "Curse" lasted from their WS win in 1918 to their next WS win in 2004.

9. Which pitcher was the first to ever pitch twenty strikeouts in a single nine inning game and was one of Boston greatest pitchers ever?

Answer: Roger Clemens

On April 29, 1986, Roger Clemens retired twenty batters in a game against the Seattle Mariners. He was the first person to do so. He was also the first person to do it twice in their career, as he completed the feat again in 1996 against the Detroit Tigers. This was one of his last games as a member of the Red Sox.

10. Who was the first person to pitch for Boston in 1901 and is considered the greatest pitcher ever?

The correct answer was Cy Young

Cy Young began his pitching career with the Cleveland Spiders in 1890. He moved to Boston on their opening season in 1901. He played for a total of 21 years and broke many records during his career. After he died in 1955, an award was created and named after him and is given to the best pitcher in both the National League and the American League each year.

Trivia Quiz - With Everything Red Sox

1. In 1917, Ernie Shore of the Red Sox pitched a "perfect" game in relief of Babe Ruth after the Babe was ejected. Who was the umpire that ejected him?

Brick Owens

Bill McKinley

Cal Hubbard

It was neither of these umpires.

2. How many Red Sox hitters hit 50 or more home runs in the 20th century?

1

2

0

3

3. From the inception of the American League in 1901 to its 100th season in 2000, how many AL championships can the Red Sox lay claim to?

11

8

10

9

4. Which colorful Red Sox player once said, "I thought we were all family here. If you're family, you don't trade your relatives to Cleveland."

Dennis Eckersley

Bernie Carbo

Bill Lee

Tony Armas

5. How many different Red Sox players claimed American League batting titles in a 25 year span, between 1979 and 2003?

6

2

0

5

6. The Red Sox started a tradition in 1960 by playing a home game on Patriots' Day, also the same day as the Boston Marathon. However, there have been a few seasons in which this game was not played. Of which of the following years did tradition hold true, and the game was played?

1995

1965

1981

1967

7. In 1990, the Red Sox traded future National League MVP Jeff Bagwell for which player?

Lee Smith

Mike Boddicker

Larry Andersen

Herm Winningham

8. How many Red Sox players can lay claim to hitting 40 or more home runs in one season, and have four or less letters in their last

name during the 20th century?

4

1

2

3

9. Who was the only Red Sox player in the 1990s to hit two home runs in the same inning?

Mo Vaughn

Ellis Burks

Nomar Garciparra

Tom Brunansky

10. In 1992, a Red Sox pitcher actually threw a no-hitter in a losing cause. Who was he?

Roger Clemens

Joe Hesketh

Tom Bolton

Matt Young

ANSWERS

1. In 1917, Ernie Shore of the Red Sox pitched a "perfect" game in

relief of Babe Ruth after the Babe was ejected. Who was the umpire that ejected him?

The correct answer was Brick Owens

It was Brick Owens who gave the Babe the thumb. After Ruth loudly complained about his strike zone following a four pitch base-on-balls, he threatened to punch Owens in the face. While Ruth made good on his promise following the ejection, Shore calmly went out to pitch. The runner on first was caught stealing, and Shore retired the next 26 in a row.

2. How many Red Sox hitters hit 50 or more home runs in the 20th century?

The correct answer was 1

Jimmie Foxx slugged 50 home runs in 1938, and was the only one to match the mark for Boston in the whole century.

3. From the inception of the American League in 1901 to its 100th season in 2000, how many AL championships can the Red Sox lay claim to?

Answer: 10

The Red Sox claimed American League titles in 1903, 1904, 1912, 1915, 1916, 1918, 1946, 1967, 1975, and 1986.

4. Which colorful Red Sox player once said, "I thought we were all family here. If you're family, you don't trade your relatives to Cleveland."

Answer: Bill Lee

Bill Lee was a fine control pitcher who played from 1969 to 1982, mostly with the Red Sox. His "Spaceman" nickname was derived from some of his more off-kilter remarks, such as wondering what they do with the Green Monster between games, and admitting he sprinkled marijuana on his cereal. This quote comes from the 1978 transaction that shipped Bernie Carbo to the Indians. He also said, "Today just cost us the pennant", and he actually walked out on the team for a day.

5. How many different Red Sox players claimed American League batting titles in a 25 year span, between 1979 and 2003?
The correct answer was 6

They are Fred Lynn, Carney Lansford, Wade Boggs, Nomar Garciaparra, Manny Ramirez, and Bill Mueller. Boggs actually collected five batting titles on his own, while Garciaparra claimed two.

6. The Red Sox started a tradition in 1960 by playing a home game on Patriots' Day, also the same day as the Boston Marathon. However, there have been a few seasons in which this game was not played. Of which of the following years did tradition hold true, and the game was played?
Answer: 1981

The lengthy baseball strike in 1994 pushed the start of the season more than a week after the 1995 Boston Marathon. The other years listed were simply scheduled off days.

7. In 1990, the Red Sox traded future National League MVP Jeff Bagwell for which player?
Answer: Larry Andersen

Larry Andersen was an effective middle reliever for many teams during a career in which he made his big league debut in 1975, and became a major leaguer for good in 1981. He only made 16 appearances in a Red Sox uniform, including one where he received a loss in game one of the ALCS in Oakland. Jeff Bagwell has since set many Astros' records for offense.

8. How many Red Sox players can lay claim to hitting 40 or more home runs in one season, and have four or less letters in their last name during the 20th century?
Answer: 2

Jim Rice slugged 46 home runs in 1978. Jimmie Foxx actually

eclipsed the 40 home run mark 5 times, but only twice for the Sox in 1936 (41) and 1938 (50).

9. Who was the only Red Sox player in the 1990s to hit two home runs in the same inning?
Answer: Ellis Burks

He did it in August 27th, 1990, against the Indians at Fenway Park.

10. In 1992, a Red Sox pitcher actually threw a no-hitter in a losing cause. Who was he?
The correct answer was Matt Young

In the first game of a doubleheader in Cleveland, Matt Young pitched a complete game and allowed no hits in a 2-1 defeat. Incidentaly, Roger Clemens hurled a two-hit shutout in the second game, which enabled the Indians to set a dubious record: Least number of hits in a doubleheader.

Trivia Quiz – Fun Facts

1. Three of these Boston Red Sox players entered the Baseball Hall of Fame as left fielders. Which Hall of Fame member did not?

Bobby Doerr

Carl Yastrzemski

Ted Williams

Jim Rice

2. How many total World Series did Hall of Fame left fielders Ted Williams, Carl Yastrzemski, and Jim Rice win?

0

2

1

3

3. The Boston Red Sox won the World Series in 1918. In what year did they next win it?

2004

1946

1986

1967

4. Which Boston Red Sox player was the last person in Major League Baseball to bat over .400 in the 20th Century?

Wade Boggs

Jim Rice

Carl Yastrzemski

Ted Williams

5. The American League was formed in 1901 with a team in Boston. In what year did the Boston team adopt the name "Red Sox"?

1903

1901

1908

1912

6. Many players who played at least one season for the Boston Red

Sox have been inducted into the Baseball Hall of Fame. However, not all of them are depicted in the Hall wearing a Red Sox cap insignia. Which of these players has a different cap?

Ted Williams

Jim Rice

Bobby Doerr

Babe Ruth

7. Which of the three DiMaggio brothers played for the Boston Red Sox?

Dave

Joe

Dom

Vince

8. The Boston Red Sox began playing their home games at Fenway Park in 1912. Although the park has been renovated a few times, what is its signature feature?

The Lone Red Seat

The Pesky Pole

The Green Monster

The Swanboat Pond

9. Between 1918 and 1923, which Boston Red Sox owner traded or sold these players to the New York Yankees: Duffy Lewis, Dutch Leonard, Ernie Shore, Carl Mays, Babe Ruth, Waite Hoyt, Joe Dugan, and Herb Pennock (among others)?

Harry Frazee

Robert Quinn

Thomas Yawkey

John Henry

10. In 1912, the year Fenway Park opened, the Boston Red Sox won their first World Series. What team did they defeat?

New York Giants

St. Louis Cardinals

Pittsburgh Pirates

Chicago Cubs

ANSWERS

1. Three of these Boston Red Sox players entered the Baseball Hall of Fame as left fielders. Which Hall of Fame member did not?

The correct answer was Bobby Doerr

Bobby Doerr was a Red Sox second baseman from 1937-1951 (less a year off for service in World War II). He entered the Hall of Fame in 1986. Ted Williams played from 1939-1960 (less about five years off for World War II and the Korean War) and was elected to the Hall of Fame in 1966. Yaz played from 1961-1983, and was enshrined in 1989. Jim Rice played from 1974-1989 and entered the Hall of Fame in 2009. Of interest, all four played their entire major league careers with the Boston Red Sox.

2. How many total World Series did Hall of Fame left fielders Ted Williams, Carl Yastrzemski, and Jim Rice win?

The correct answer was 0

Williams got to play in only one World Series, 1946, when the Red Sox lost 4-3 to the St. Louis Cardinals. Yaz played in two World Series. In 1967, the Sox lost to the St. Louis Cardinals 4-3; in 1975, they lost to the Cincinnati Reds 4-3. Rice played in two World Series, the 1975 loss to the Reds and the 1986 loss to the New York Mets 4-3. Note the margin in each of these losses.

3. The Boston Red Sox won the World Series in 1918. In what year did they next win it?

The correct answer was 2004

After losing to the St. Louis Cardinals 4-3 in both 1946 and 1967, and the New York Mets in 1986 (also 4-3), the Red Sox defeated the Cardinals 4-0 in 2004 for their first World Series win since 1918, some 86 years!

4. Which Boston Red Sox player was the last person in Major League Baseball to bat over .400 in the 20th Century?

The correct answer was Ted Williams

On the last day of the 1941 season, with the Red Sox playing a doubleheader against the Philadelphia Athletics, Williams was batting .39955 which, rounded, would officially have been .400. Offered the chance to sit out those games, Williams refused. That day he went 6 for 8 and finished at .406. His lifetime average was .344. Boggs highest average was .368/lifetime .328. Yaz top average was .329/lifetime .285. Rice reached .325/lifetime .298. [In 1941, a sacrifice fly counted as an at-bat. Under later rules, Williams would have batted between .411 and .419.]

5. The American League was formed in 1901 with a team in Boston. In what year did the Boston team adopt the name "Red Sox"?
Answer: 1908

For the 1801-1907 seasons, Boston had no official nickname, although it was variously called such names as "The Bostons," "The Bostonians," "The Pilgrims," or "The Boston Americans." After the 1907 season, owner John Taylor selected red as the team color and "Red Sox" as the official nickname. In 1903, Boston beat Pittsburgh in the first World Series. In 1912, The Red Sox moved into Fenway Park.

6.
The correct answer was Babe Ruth

Babe Ruth has a New York Yankee cap. He played for the Boston Red Sox (1914-1919), the Yankees (1920-1934), and the Boston Braves (1935). Bobby Doerr (1937-1951 less time for military service), Ted Williams (1939-1960 less military service time), and Jim Rice (1974-1989) played their entire major league careers with the Boston Red Sox.

7. Which of the three DiMaggio brothers played for the Boston Red Sox?

The correct answer was Dom

The youngest of the three brothers, Dominic Paul "Dom" DiMaggio, called "The Little Professor," played his entire major league career (1940-1953, less World War II service) with the Red Sox. A seven-time All-Star and superior lead-off hitter, he batted over .300 four times and ended with a lifetime .298 batting average. Vincent Paul "Vince" DiMaggio, the oldest brother, played from 1937-1946, with the Boston Bees, Cincinnati Reds, Pittsburgh Pirates, Philadelphia Phillies, and New York Giants. He was twice an All-Star. Joseph Paul "Joe" DiMaggio spent his entire 13-year career (1936-1951, less World War II service) as a New York Yankee. He was an All-Star all 13 years. A member of the Hall of Fame, he played on nine World Series championship teams. All three brothers played center field![Dave DiMaggio was not one of the brothers.]

8.

Answer: The Green Monster

"The Green Monster" is the 37-foot+ high left field wall 310-315 feet from home plate that was part of the original structure. A scoreboard, manually operated, was added in 1934. It was not painted green until 1947 (before then it was full of ads). "The Pesky Pole" is the name for the pole marking the right field foul line, 302 feet from home plate. Johnny Pesky, a light-hitting shortstop and longtime Red Sox coach hit a few home runs around the pole, which in 2006, on Pesky's 87th birthday, was dedicated as "Pesky's Pole." "The Lone Red Seat" is in the right field bleachers (Section 42, Row 37, Seat 21). It marks the longest home run in the 20th century hit at Fenway Park, 502 feet by Ted Williams on June 6, 1946. [The Swanboat Pond is in Boston Common and has nothing to do with the Red Sox.]

9.

Answer: Harry Frazee

Harry H. Frazee, who owned the Red Sox from 1917-1923, destroyed what was a magnificent team. J.A. Robert Quinn owned the team from 1923-1933, when he sold it to Tom Yawkey. Yawkey, and later the Jean Yawkey Trust, had control from 1933-2002. John Henry led a group that gained ownership in 2002. It was still in control in 2015.

10. In 1912, the year Fenway Park opened, the Boston Red Sox won

Answer: New York Giants

The Red Sox defeated the Giants 4-3, with one tie. The Series was hotly contested. In Game One, at the Polo Grounds, the Sox won 4-

3. Game Two, at Fenway Park, ended in a 6-6 tie after 11 innings. In Game Three at Fenway Park, the Giants prevailed 2-1. Game Four was at the Polo Grounds; the Sox won 3-1. Game Five was played in Boston, with the Sox winning 2-1, giving them a 3-1 advantage. At the Polo Grounds, the Giants beat the Red Sox 5-2 in Game Six. At Fenway Park, in Game Seven, the Giants routed the Sox 11-4. In Game Eight, the Red Sox edged the Giants 3-2 in ten innings, coming back after the Giants scored a run to go ahead in the top of the 10th.

Printed in Dunstable, United Kingdom

70783433R00031